Facing High Water

Facing High Water

John Brandi

White Pine Press / Buffalo, New York

Published by
White Pine Press
P.O. Box 236
Buffalo, New York 14201
www.whitepine.org

Cover collage and chapter adornments by John Brandi

First Edition

ISBN 978-1-893996-22-9

Printed and bound in the United States of America

Library of Congress Control Number: 2008928422

The author wishes to thank the editors of the following publications where
some of these poems first appeared: *Air Mail, Big Bridge, The Café Review,
Celestial Graffiti, The Harwood Anthology, Looking Back to Place, Natural
Bridge, New Magazine* (Paris), *Sin Fronteras: Writers without Borders,* and
the *Santa Fe New Mexican.* "Time is Short," "Work Song While
Gardening," "Looking for Water," and "Staying on Course" were issued as
limited-edition, letterpress broadsides by Jerry Reddan at Tangram Press.
"Walking with Frank O'Hara and Po Chü-i" appeared as a broadside pro-
duced by Steve Simpson. I am indebted to Just Buffalo Literary Center and
White Pine Press for a residency in Buffalo, N.Y. through their World of
Voices literature series, funded by the John R. Oishei Foundation.

Gratitude to Renée Gregorio and Ed Kissam for their suggestions during
the final stages of this book; to Ámbar Past for a house in Chiapas; to the
people of Cuba, ever generous and welcoming; to Ponheary Li in Angkor
Wat; to Maura, Guatam, Ranjan, Vasudha, and Mishti in Kolkata.

Special acknowledgment to Giovanna Brandi and William Wicks
for their generous support towards this publication.

To the poets, musicians, artists,
and free-spirited thinkers who have left us for the beyond.
May your voices continue to invigorate, encourage,
transform, and sustain us.

Contents

I.

Living in the Mountains

Troubled waters are frozen fast.
Under clear heaven, moonlight & shadow ebb & flow.

Murasaki Shikibu

I Lift the Wine, Put My Eye to the Glass

The mountains are clear today,
    easy to see far, so few people.
Spring grasses whistle, a few cherry blossoms
   float down. Shreds of rain hang from gathering clouds.
Under the eave, purple shadows on yellow sand,
    smell of split cedar, strong.

What did I do today?
Watch the magpies return, spade the squash,
    line my shoes on the porch and polish them,
rewrap the hose into a perfect circle?

Got a few ideas, didn't jot them down.
    Tried to count how many days old I am.
Got up to 21,900, but quickly decided, on a day like today,
       better to wet the brush and play,
let the mind become a whirlpool
      —spin clear, and dance.

Tomorrow, maybe go back to the page,
    fix the spacing in the fence rails,
replace the hinges on the gate. But, this evening,
another cup of wine before I rise from the chair,
    lift my arms to the darkening sky,

see the shape of lights coming on,
    little yellow squares in a distant house.
And then, walk into the field, watch my feet turn green,
   watch the mountains change shape
       with each step I take.

Evening Poem

Mend the shed, watch clouds
fill the sky. Let my hair go, my head
reflect the light. Who cares—

Hot wind, cold feet,
straw between the teeth, dirt on the gloves.
Moon over the farmer still out there on the rake.
    Nothing permanent, same old battle.

Bills scattered, dust on the shelves.
Rice in the bag, letters to post.
    A new set of rules, a six-pack of whims?

Let the pinecones fall where they fall,
    the crickets live in their corners.

Nothing waits out there, no big award.
Not even enough ink in the pen to sign a few books
    —but there's a line of cranes, and under them,
        the up and down bray of a donkey.

Listen, there's a house
halfway up the mountain. Nobody lives there,
                just the thunder.

Why not learn to walk on clouds?
If you return from the dream, let me know
if only the crazy walk the night
    in broken cliffs, where lightning
            sets fire to pine.

Walking with Frank O'Hara and Po Chü-i

1.

Who sees the green heron
roosting at the river's mouth? Frank points it out,
along with a bed spring in the reeds, and a can full of teeth.

Po Chü-i leans on his stick, praises fox and clam,
the friendship of fools, the speed at which a mountain
becomes river, and water sand.

The bridge gives a creak, sun rolls up its sleeves.
There's a wine shop down the road where Frank makes a call
on the public telephone. "Lordy," I hear him say,

"So many echoes in my head, I blame it on Blake
or the latitude of the stars," while Po Chü-i takes a leak
against a cinnamon tree, muttering

"Why hoard gold to build a perfect country home,
when here far from crowds, there's all this spring light
owned by no one?"

2.

Up trail, snow dusting our shoulders,
we brew clear tea from a roaring stream. The border's closed
but Po Chü-i gets drunk with the gatekeeper

and when he sleeps, slips through the threshold
to the Forbidden Land, refines his gaze and rises late,
knowing how useful it is to be useless.

Down slope, Frank's on his back
counting bats in the Hall of Temporary Progress.
    "A great feast of upside-down dreams!"

3.

Just after midnight a warm breeze
brings blossoms to the camellia tree.
Alone, all I hear is the settling of the eaves.

The company that's kept me
has gone off into scattered clouds. I'll get up now,
untwist the wild rose from the gate,

leave it open for Po Chü-i and Frank
to come some other night. My clothes are thin
    —the going was never easy.

So many drives and compulsions,
but now the moon is full, the belly content
to be empty.

The friendship of fools is sweet
as the last grapes on the vine. A thousand tree rings
from now, what more will survive?

Early Evening, Gazing East

Apricots in blossom, moon aligned with Pleiades.
An old friend, out there somewhere
gone adrift on new soil.

Above coal smoke and human babble
he eats wind, bites icicles from the eaves to brew his tea.
Looking into the dust of humankind, he sees
dead rivers, crowded stations, pandas and moon bear
miserably caged, million dollar high rise
       gleaming in stale air.

Traveling deeper, he spies the tracks
of something small—sable or marten—disappearing
into a snowdrift under a ledge of silver moss.
His boots are broken, his hands red.
Saliva leaks from the corners of his mouth.

He'll follow fireflies into bracken, chew bitter resins
to clear the senses, even it out
where things have no price, sleep in a farmhouse
tonight, everything up to the wind.

Has the Old Homeland Changed?

1.

Unrest has sent me to the hills.
Senseless babbling from the capital, armies spreading
east and west   —for whose glory?

A neighbor knocks on my door.
She's got apricots and peaches, I've got extra squash
and spearmint from the stream.

The wind is sweet, berries ripe.
Up high where clouds fill the pass, old age
has brought me longer life.

2.

Down below, it's all on fire.
People grasp at inflated dreams, take refuge
in lies that catch like burrs on every promise.

Why not hang dried fruit on a string,
bathe in whitewater, loosen the robe
and enjoy the dark?

Haste leaves no time for song.
The deeply troubled turn away from truth,
fan the flames at the slightest spark.

3.

Setting posts in the breeze,
a few words roll between my teeth.
I let the taste come clear,

fine food for an empty stomach:
these overgrown roads, bridge planks
frosty, the season sharp.

A lizard darts out, a snake tucks in.
A short snooze in the weeds
and I'm back on track.

4.

Only a few love the untrimmed path
where cliffs rise into cold blue sky
as hot dust flies.

When the barbarians pass their next law
and come spying on me,
there'll be no one home.

I'm glad for these rocky slopes, neighbors
I know, this backcountry
                —lonely and full.

Cloud Pilgrim
for Renée

Years into months into days.
The garden shines with evening rain.

A little wine, who cares if the footbridge
has missing planks?

We move closer, go barefoot
in the cosmos. Wander far, never leave the gate.

Ten years, the lotus opening.
Ten years, the zigzag trail to the Perfume Temple.

A pair of crows flies home at dusk.
A pair of children runs into the field.

Full, rowdy voices,
blue smoke down canyon.

Your taste and mine, one glass, one drink,
one hundred flowers, a thousand cricket songs.

Ten thousand days with you
in the Eye of Heaven.

Weminuche Wilderness, Late August

Throw open the tent flap,
cold drizzle last night. The river talks softly
between mountain grass.

Frozen dew brightens the camp ring,
fingers of mist follow a rockslide into the sun.

Slipping on a sweater,
I mutter to my skeleton: "You've gotten thin!"

Bluebells, fireweed dance in sudden draft.
Aspen fire crackles, smoke dips
                into the valley.

"But what I nurture here
never grows thin," said old master Ch'ien.

A smile breaks over my face
                —this wild land!

Having looked in this direction
who could ever turn back?

Missing a Good Friend Gone Far
for Bari Long

Perhaps this letter will cross
with one from you, catch fire in heaven, find its way
to your brushwood shack, the boiling roots and seeping tea.

Maybe you're on your way back, throat singing
with a Mongolian bride. Or gone further in,
rattling the two heads of your drum,
riding auroras of timeless light.

Here, I'm saturated with papers and ink,
empty tracks this way and that. Snow on chokecherries,
broken roof to let in the breeze.

The whole country's on its knees, manipulated
with threats of an invisible enemy. Everything I want to say
is subject to exam, letters opened, words scanned.

My shoes are off, too heavy with mud.
I'll postmark this from a cave, with a willow stick
dipped in cinnabar.

Write me in return, or come see me
after you've gone deeper, your chin full of hair,
your eyes grown out of your head.

Waiting for Snow

While creeks go silent with rusty stones,
I kindle twigs in the stove, watch flowers fade,
sugar crystallize in trailing vines.

As if on queue, chairs move closer to hearth,
jade plants wander in from the porch,
light angles low on the shed.

Books open, pen lifts into hand.
A jay hangs upside down and feasts on a sunflower.
    The old barn belches and sags in the cold.

All that I love is wrapped in solitude:
tin roofs, juniper woods, clay ovens and coyote dens,
fence lines fox-trotting off the horizon.

To think no one's battling each other
out there almost seems true —and I want it to be,
    want the world covered in an avalanche of moans,

the kind that go with love,
music the color of grenadine, revolution rising
through the clear strings of dawn.

But the sky is dark now,
words burn in a wreath around my skull.
    Ice crawls up the glass, snow fills the silence.

Tonight, only dry crackle of oak
and these fingers that dig through darkness
    to right what has toppled.

At It Again

I know I'm here
inside the middle of day, at my desk
like an island at sea, the universe spinning on its own,
snow peaks sliding into waves, food running low.

I know I'm here—as are the bones,
    the fence rails whimpering in the wind,
air hanging low in the valley—to become smaller
until I lean from my tears and break clear tracks
        through ignorance and neglect.

It's another winter day near zero
    and I'm in the loft of minor deeds,
between the double space of keys and knocking questions,
    but I can hear the cricket say its name, see a star
in the center of day, hear the spoon stir in its drawer,
a knife unbutton the sash
        from the clumsy bride of joy.

I know who bites who,
that there's rage over the hill,
        that darkness is not opaque.

You don't have to tell me a seed waits
beneath this hard soil, that somewhere beyond
another world holds us in shape, a hammer rings
as the eaves gather ice, as the weather shifts
        and the birds take flight.

Staying on Course

In the face of turmoil, there's strength
in the quiet life. Dipping a pail into the current
where the river turns white, clearing old growth,
     leaving the primrose tangled just so.

Here where wood smoke drifts
from chimneys, the eye follows a goldfinch
    into cedar hollows. A full spring creek plays
for the ear. A child learns to weave,
       a man walks and never drives.

Today I roll out paper, break off twigs,
    sketch the meandering bindweed,
loosen my clothes, clear the head,
      let the gate squeak in the breeze.

After so many acts of resistance,
      getting angrier in a crazed world,
it feels good to weed dead grass
   from purple shoots, and bolster my courage
        for the next round.

I find unexpected exhilaration
sorting flowers from tangled vines,
      drinking right from the spring
I've put down a few poems
     as they've come.

II.

A Rose for Lorca

Sueño, fermento y sueño.
Este es el mundo, amigo—

Federico García Lorca

A Rose for Lorca

A little girl in white chiffon
pinned with the Sacred Heart skips hopscotch squares,
her feet two asterisks in the lemon-colored rain.
And she is how it would look, I imagine,
my own soul, if it could escape my coat and walk this world
    of bells and peeling facades.

On Media Luna she passes a man
selling mouse traps under José Martí on a white stallion.
At the docks, where Lorca sat amid heartbreak
and sweetened rum, she joins the queue for the ferry
at the Pier of Light —bicycles, ball caps, spandex hips,
printing ink and fresh carnations on the breeze,
    Santa Barbara showing her worth in see-though snakeskin,
the face of Ché over blood oranges and waving cane.

Green air, green eyes in copper faces,
pilgrims crossing the bay to the shrine of Yemayá,
and this girl, head tilted to the luxurious warmth of the sea,
fills me with the innocuous heat of Cuba:
    fragile liberty, eternal back slap,
        strong coffee always waiting.

On the opposite shore, a lighthouse tilts
in seismic frenzy, moves all boundaries, delivers
a hundred spinning trumpets from the sky. A red bell clangs,
a donkey saddled with gladiolas clatters up the plank.
    The ferry moves off, and the girl in white
becomes a heatwave, a star lost among tunnels
of sweat and perfume, thick chatter

of politics and apocalypse.

In the ringing and shuffling, she is there
with that perfect look of a transparent diamond
—a rose in the teeth of the sea.

Muelle de la Luz, Havana

Where the Bus Left Us

This is where the tide rolled up its sleeves,
where the old painter added wings to weightlifters
and made nipples rise under women's lace.

This is where the gun ships put in
and darkness opened its eye with fire, where Batista
followed Machado, and the CIA planned its blood wedding
for the unshaven men in dull green.

This is where confetti bombed the windscreen
of Mario's pink Edsel, and the bride wore red
under a flame tree. This is the little guy in the big drink,
drums thumping, chains rattling.

This is the side of life that bends your elbows to the sun
from the lap of the holy mother, whose black seashells
and gourd rasp shatter the blockade with song.

This is where cold rain brightens our backs
as the patron saints dance under children waving blue flags
on yellow verandas to the armada of black suits
ninety miles across the waves.

Paseo de Martí, Havana

A Dance Hall in Baracoa
(with a line from Vicente Aleixandre)

It's the hour without hands
where clocks become stars and truth books its desire
    under damp skirts billowing with combustion.

It's night without faith in tomorrow,
masts unfurling as the deck fills with rolling hips
    rhythming to the pounding wails of the band
belting it out over guitars and bongos, a stand-up bass
    washed in by the waves, a guy going crazy
on improvised maracas (a pair of toilet-bowl floats
                            filled with pebbles).

It's the captain at the wheel
steering the rudder with a contagious spark
as he delivers his punch in counterpoint euphoria,
    his face with the aura of pure pleasure, legs sliding
through the foaming swamp of ingot-hot dancers,
one with an electric ruby blinking between her cleavage,
    another shiny with sweat in thigh-revealing skirt,
heels smoking as she dips beneath the arm
of her rumba king, her perfumed stem
        leaning into the open sway of his tree.

It's the stampede of breath through flared nostrils,
    shoulder-to-shoulder exile of body into fire
as the songster's voice drops from smooth, loquacious notes
        to a smoky rasp of sex and growl.

Eyes closed, he's gone
    into resplendent Eden, doing the splits
with an elegant knows-her-business silver-haired señora
    who maneuvers her steps as if she were 25,
shaking into an erotic spin around the old singer
        who minute by minute gets younger *—Baila!*

Everyone's buzzing with rum at the center of a flower
    like birds, maybe like angels, like those green angels
        who have lived in water.

It Was When

The book seller in the Plaza de Armas
took a small volume of Nicolás Guillén from paperweights
and blotting paper, and belted out
    "Digo que yo no soy un hombre puro"
  drawing smiles from policemen in the shade, and a nod
from the driver of a powder-blue Nomad,
        sunflowers around a black saint in the rear seat.

It was when the children ran to the meringue man
whistling his goods from a cardboard box, and the bartender
stepped from swinging shutters to feed the donkey
  scuffing its heel at the door.

It was when the laundry lady pinned a smile
over a line of brassieres in the Ambos Mundos Hotel
where Hemingway stood naked at his typewriter
  pounding out *For Whom the Bell Tolls.*

It was when the earth opened and trumpets took charge,
and the child at her marbles looked between
        my hurried legs and asked *"What* are you?"
that I knew I'd never bring myself home the same.

I'd listen for the fist through the window, a storm of feet
on the balcony, I'd fire the first shot
for love, I'd embrace the enemy—
              the one outside, the one in me.

Meditations at the Pier of Light

We need to unmake the bed, stir the coals
bring in the edges, see farther than the eyes.

We need to undo our robes, face the black whole
We need neighborly Creole, pull-the-plug Speakeasy
blue light against gold facades.

We need great works of art signed without names
slow saxophone boleros, mambo daybreak
legs spinning under hiked-up skirts

a procession in full swing
heels of fire tapping sorrow free.

Anything, Compadre

Give me something to begin with.
    A whisper rearranging itself in the dust,
stones in action christening a river bed,
        bones sliding back and forth in love.

Give me your deck,
your spinning compass, flags of surf
    washing the mouths of the devout.

I will not die with this false passport
they've given me. I do not support the empirical plot
to rearrange other countries. My imagination
        is a burning raindrop.

Give me a hammer, I'll smash the wall.
Give me your unsold dumplings, the scissors,
    the bucket, the marigolds your sister died with
in the bombed market.

I want to water her sacrificed body,
    hold her struggle between my shoulders,
the heart cracked with fear.

Give me your shivering piano,
    the child subject to dizzy spells,
the grandmother whose blown-out eardrums
        hear the force of betrayal.

Give me music, its shoreless weeping,
    the smell of a newborn, the taste of an oasis
in the throat —anise, pine shavings,
    the deep iron of love.

Let me wake, and know my exact place
in the struggle. Roughen me up.
      See what I can take, so that I know
how much I can give.

Teaching in the Rust Belt

1.

In the rain, children of immigrants
are eating bread from newsprint, their mothers
in thick collars warming hands around paper cups of coffee
under stone churches whose eyes are black with years of carbon
from factories long shut, now revamped by city planners
    into art spaces and attorneys' quarters.

Clouds roll in with heavy tomorrows,
rusty bridges blink in the weeds and snow, cables hanging
    over jagged ice where men with furnace eyes
patrol the borders with blue pistols and throats of gravel.

As I walk into International School #142,
sign in, get my tag, and am told to remove my cap
    (as I once had to do when teaching in prisons),
I hear a mix of English and Vietnamese, languages
from Somalia, Laos, Albania.

Climbing the stairs, I'm engulfed in waves of black,
sienna, mahogany; a glistening undertow of beaded dreads,
head scarves, white Nikes, savage islands
    of swinging buttocks, smooth arms heavy
with textbooks and graffitied binders.

And I am to listen and respond,
slide in and out of dialogue created by these curious
thumping brains, these names hardly pronounceable;
    some gentle, some in shade, some tumbling down
into the ice ages of the modern world.

2.

As the days progress, my chest hammers
with brown rivers and delirious jungles, desert wars
    and refugee camps. The uncertainty of shattered
neighborhoods, families broken and maimed
riding death carts to every corner of the planet.

But these young people, of so many colors
and languages, will not stand for deception, nor bleed
with the promises of the elite. They write to bring
    in the crop of each other's dreams.

Semaj admits he gets more mileage
with his new name, and is already getting better
at love poems. "My rhymes are wicked
    and I'm not so full of myself."
Ebony tells me, "I like reading your poems
    backwards, they're easier that way."

And though it is April and snowing,
we are together under clear sky, smashing borders
   with words. One writes about a bird's exploding nest
in a garden she mistook for refuge.
Another of his pastor's daughter who hung herself
    by a coat wire in a closet of smashed desire.

Someone brings fire from silk sleeves.
Someone walks us through piles of rubbish to a first kiss
        in a chopped-up alley whining with sirens.
The young man from Niger says a book's in his head
bigger than he's ever read,

waiting without guilt to come undone.

The girl from Dai Lanh is happy to know
   I love green papaya salad with cold beer
in the heat of her homeland. Her poem smells of cinnamon
   and burnished gold. In the pixels of her screen there's a path
uphill where hope carries truth far out
     into the silver apron of the South China Sea.

Raphaela asks me to read *In What Disappears*
   because, she says, "all weekend I've read it over and over
and don't know what it means, but love how it makes
   me feel." Yes, I tell her, I'd be happy to, just for you.
And that a poet named William Carlos Williams
   once said, "Sometimes a poem doesn't want
     to be understood, it just wants to be."

3.

The old school room, an embarrassment
of water stains and taped pipes, is suddenly luminous
   like those ingots of steel from dead foundries
out the caged window. And I'm shivering and inebriated
   with this bond in the face of regimes who manipulate
fear for political ends, and divide and disunify
   as a matter of policy to achieve their ends.

To battle the shadow of doom
   these students write the sexiest poems.
They are soft and generous, with claws that purr
   under the skin. They are fierce as dynamite
blasting through slabs of marble as they unlock

love and longing from secret cobwebs
    that burn with nocturnal fever.

Brick by brick they undo the drowned rooms,
    the curbed tangles, and brick by brick
my assumptions go as they raze the building
    until no wall stands. And the gates of revolution
are under the veil that lifts from Fadwa's face, asking
    "Are there ever days when words surround you
    like they are alive and you just want to be
      with them as long as they'll let you?"

I know, in the blood beating
in these voices, that poetry is alive and well
    when Ramon says, "I don't write for people
who wear gloves." Or when Ira says, "Not so tough
as to be overdone, but not so raw as to be dripping."
Or when the girl with clouds in the door of her heart,
twisting a jade Buddha at her neck,
    stands in front of the class and sums it all up:

"A poem is when you burn with something
    that makes fences fall and you are alone with the night,
      free to see the stars, free to talk with the one
inside you who sees what no one else knows."

Buffalo, New York

III.

Setting the Boat Adrift

*Sometimes a man stands up during supper
and walks outdoors, and keeps on walking,
because of a church that stands somewhere in the East.*

Rilke

Li River Song

Beautiful this morning.
Green hills evaporate in mist,
tombs under tangerine trees smoke in the sun.

Yellow roads, yellow faces,
yellow clay between the potter's hands.

A woman gathers morning glories,
knows I'm here, but doesn't look up as I pass.

I will take the trail to Heaven's Gate,
watch gibbons play, fish for words at the waterwheel,
scatter fresh grass   —and nap.

Beautiful ancient feel
of cloud and dragon, breeze turning red
as it stirs through the lacquered pavilion.

Empty and full, with nowhere to go,
how civil to trade work for laziness,

lose the path, and wake
with flowers inside my hat.

Guangxi, China

Traveling Deeper

(with a line from Wang Wei)

Everyone's headed to market town,
deeper and deeper, where mountains close in
and houses are adzed and pegged. Where blue rivers
    match women's turquoise earrings
and bridges straddle whitewater
        like miniature wooden castles.

Geese to trade, ripe berries, too.
Yokes and plow handles, tofu pressed in wooden baskets,
30 proof wine in a plastic can, a cartwheel tied
    to the bus roof, banging up and down.
Everyone headed to market town,

where canyons narrow
  and stone terraces climb the sky,
where young peddlers sell eggs from their sleeves,
    and the prettiest women
carry the biggest knives.

Come, ride a dragonfly into tangled vines,
    tilt your head under a shot of apricot wine.
Watch the moon undress, let green mist wet your sleeves.
  Be content, and be generous. *All across the pond,*
        dew pearls flutter and whirl
            on the lotus leaves.

Guizhou, China

Downwind in a Drifting Boat

Fish line tangled
between broken stumps, rings of smoke
above the woods.

Insects cry from willow reeds,
a hundred rambling shacks hide in mist.

Float, let the destination ebb,
    the waft of jasmine is dark and warm.

But who of stillbirth
bleeds in shadows, who of torture
is silent in the trees?

Rags, old age at forty,
a few sticks to light the fire.

In the evening wind
    something catches in the dark
and slows our boat.

Nam Khong, Laos

Nostalgia

For the world before it was,
eyes rolling into the body's garden
with the heat of each other's tree.
Tongues leaving light
between the teeth.

Radiance
in the heart of each man I meet.
Zero take over, no greed.
Mediocrity muzzled, indifference
given the guillotine.

Undammed rivers
the poet laureates of our time.
Wind in wood shavings, whales in sea spray,
water exploding in stone.

The song of humans,
unhurried, wandering in and out
the gate, enough time
between work
to play.

Phnom Penh

I hear a lullaby through the wall
as I bring your calloused feet up to my shoulders,
take your darkness inside me, burn with you.

And when we are done, I walk
the streets, brave, bruised with your aroma,
filled with exploding rain.

Hang deceit from the balcony!
let it bleach in the wind. I want laughter again,
jump ropes whirling over polished stone.

I want the saddest pleasure,
the insistent wreck, the slow blade of infinity
to announce our names.

Angkor Wat

Among crumbled pavilions, steam rises
from sun-warmed bodies of dancing apsaras
who float from stone with trance-like smiles.

A song drifts in from a swept-earth clearing
beyond a collapsed wall where a singer, her eyes closed,
sits in a circle of musicians, each with an alms bowl
and an unstrapped plastic leg at his side.
        Survivors, all of them, from the Khmer Rouge.

Nearby, a bas relief shows a king humbling a woman
on a bed of arrows. Our guide explains: "The story is
that the king subdued the woman to prove his strength,
but he should have sacrificed his power
            to show his strength   —not the woman."

Our guide too is a victim of the Khmer Rouge,
taken from her family, forced to dig her own grave, clubbed
and left for dead before finally escaping.

Under an empty niche that once held
a meditating Buddha, she talks about world leaders,
their inability to conquer greed.
        "War everywhere," she says—

"Even if you win
    you have the word 'lost' inside."

Visiting a Taoist Recluse

It's the road through the clouds
above the sacred lake along wooded cliffs
under the lap of Kanchendzonga.

It's the sky-blue veranda
lined with copper wheels spinning mantras
into crystal void.

It's the Old Scholar stepping from
his timeless shack, a playful smile
at the world's edge, a fox barking
          from the gorge below.

It's his daughter, roused from sleep—
Tara herself, serving cookies and snow-melt tea
under the big umbrella he's plucked down
to give us shade, while grandkids
          do handstands in the sun.

It's solitude's indispensable power,
clean lines on the face of one who's settled in mind.
Water from the source, fire in the ring,
   a loose-fitting robe fit for dance.

Summer grass, winter frost—
a steady climb between rock and fern.
That's how we got here,
   lost again where trails grow thin.

Among Higher Beings

The hill shrine overlooking Kathmandu
is circled with prayer wheels worked by monkeys
who spill between priests to shoplift pilgrims' offerings.

Into the trees they swing, clutching rupees
and incense, laughing as they wipe their faces
    with sacred banners stolen from marble altars.

When shadows mince the valley, the monkeys descend
and sit with tourists to avail themselves for consultations.
  Under the moon, they discuss the calamities of the world,
ours, not theirs, gone amok amid warlords of deceit
    caught in eternal rebirth of never knowing better.

Monkeys, hairy and bare-balled
in their airborne picnic through abstract conceptions,
take no refuge in satori or redemption.
They stay naked, do it in doorways without contract
or divorce, and slip from view beating breasts
    without need for laptop, lawsuits,
        cellular climax or call waiting.

The highest being has the longest tail.
    No reason for checkbook, surgical transplant
      or thirst-vomiting ego.

As we sleep, monkeys retreat,
stare invisibly, their green banners flying,
    their clear, knowing eyes opening with sobs
      to haunt our reckless pillage.

The Chai Wallah's Story

In a narrow alley opposite the Well of Knowledge
I take a seat at a curbside table, order tea, and ponder
the inevitable question   —Why India?

Wrapped in soliloquy, I fail to acknowledge
the chai wallah who wipes the table and froths a long spout
of cardamom-spiced tea into my cup.

Obsessed with maintaining my thoughts,
I fumble for change, and pay the man without looking up.
But the chai wallah doesn't move   —his stained white apron
visible from the corner of my eye.

When I finally give a glance, he's standing like an idol
smoking a tiny cigarette through a hole in his forehead,
letting smoke rings slip from his mouth.

"A terrible misfortune," he explains.
"I was shot during a train robbery near Allahabad.
By the will of the Divine Guru, I survived. But not without
this unsightly wound. I've made the best of it, though.
I use my tragedy to attract business, to amuse people like you.

At that moment I realized   —Why India?
Here one discovers in reality what one usually
finds only in dreams.

The chai wallah took the cigarette from his forehead,
examined my tip, and tilted his head in that odd Indian way
where what looks like No really means Yes.
As he entered the kitchen, he suddenly turned:

"A person who accepts his fate
just as nature puts it to him gets along fine
in this world   —and in the next."

Varanasi, India

The Gem Ghetto

1.

The man brought out two cups of tea
and left me on my own over a tray of precious stones,
a shaft of sun from a tiny window lighting the counter
        where I put my fingers into a sparkling pyramid
of rubies, sapphire, and finely-cut lapis.

Because he had temporarily excused himself
and because I knew the city was known for lacing tourists' tea
        with sleep-inducing drugs, I switched the proprietor's cup
with the one he'd given me, not realizing he knew I'd do this
and had laced his own cup with the drug I'd hoped to avoid.

When he returned with silver-foiled sweetmeats
        and sugar-coated fennel seeds, I watched his head
slightly dismantle from his body,
        his smile wander over me in a fog,
and while my rickshaw wallah waited outside,
I drowsily accepted whatever bargain the merchant offered:
glass garnets, plastic topaz, beautiful polyurethane rubies,
even crystals of arsenic sulfide, bits of meteor
        and flashing synthetic tetrahedrons
                                of green tourmaline.

2.

When I came to, I was in the bus station
        under a clock with a smiling Bombay movie star,
missing my wristwatch and belt, but I had my diamonds,
        suspiciously light in their tiny plastic box,
and fine beads of fools gold wrapped

53

in the smudged ink of my travelers checks.

The station smelled of exhaust and hot peanuts.
The fat man frying somozas, and his toothless mother
by the door were not counterfeit, nor were the heatwaves
over the sleeping baby or the priest
picking his teeth on his straw mat.

As the bus arived and people pushed aboard,
I found my place among suits and saris
and sap-stained legs, while out the window
              a rooster began to crow.

It was there I realized, as I waited
for the journey to begin and my drowsed head to clear,
that there will always exist, between charm and truth,
the monkery and jive of the human nod over false stones,
while the gods glitter in their niches
and the cosmic abacus clacks up the cost
         of trust and ignorance.

3.

I felt a little better, I suppose,
even smiled as the bus turned its chrome eyelids
to the vast dry hills. I opened a book and rolled my money
into a shoe   —where it would be safe,
as the earth turned dark, and one by one
     the lights of passing villages came on.

Agra, India

How to Proceed to the Marriage Bed

A priest sits cross legged in a wooden temple
whisking flies from silver-foiled sweets. Above him,
carved into the ceiling, amorous couples writhe and copulate,
bodies brightened with lapis and cinnabar.

A maiden brings a mendicant between her breasts
and his staff bursts into flowers. A mother suckles her child
as her husband takes her from behind. Two courtesans watch
with lowered eyelids, hips thrust out, skirts undone.

The inner sanctum is hazy with incense,
marked with red handprints. On the altar, inside a wheel
of figures gasping with pleasure, Shiva penetrates Shakti,
Imagination wraps her legs around Wisdom.

Here, the priest pours milk over a lingam, offers trays
of burning camphor to women who fan fire to their shoulders.
    Here, a mirror is epoxied with a pair of scissors
over a sign that reminds the pilgrim:

"If one cannot cut the knots of shame, hate, and fear
one may not proceed to the marriage bed
        —nor to the house of the gods."

Bhaktapur, Nepal

Hiding Eros

1.

Central Java

Among stone ruins amid moist tangles
of vine, the Goddess without Shame is carved
in smooth basalt where springs flow from dark earth
and locusts sing. She dates from Vedic times
      and always appears like this —undressed,
         legs pulled back, her triangle swollen.

Half hidden down a slippery trail,
she sanctifies massive roots of sacred groves
where each cloud-forest tree is venerated
as a storage vessel of rain. In her elemental birthing posture
she is the Essential Female —receptive, creative,
         synonymous with water.

Freshly wetted, deliciously ripe,
she's been sprinkled with jasmine by village women
   who, though they profess the faith of the Prophet,
are animist by nature, the old fertility cult
      shining nakedly through the veil of religion.

2.

Northern Cambodia

Through wooded hills
to the source of a small river, auspicious shudder
of insects, steely vibrations from outcrops of stone.

Where the overgrowth opens:
    an ancient Hindu site. Countless lingams carved
into the riverbed, designed to sanctify the water
as it flows over them,
      then down onto the flats to irrigate the rice.

Unlike the temples of India,
no priests are needed to perform the ritual
of pouring water over lingams to consecrate them.
Here, water crowns from moist leafage, gives a cry,
        then sings over the stone on its own.

I quarry a pebble from the depths,
shake its wetness into the sun, roll it around
in my mouth, hide the taste
      —let it carry me into the world.

3.

Bali

Before dawn, Kade is already at the spigot
filling her pots, her body translucent under the white veins
of the Milky Way. She and Pak Wayan built their house
here, above the sacred confluence of the River Oos.

On a ledge below the house
a huge banyan shades a stone temple
tiered with thatch, incense smoking from each corner.

Pak says, "We straightened the world a few years ago
with a big ceremony here.
                    Now we need another."

Below the temple, exactly where the two legs
of the River Oos join, a highly-venerated Venus mound
of slick basalt rises from the water, glistening with moss.

Eros reveals herself in this liquid nave
bordered with ginger and datura. She lets the river take her,
        untamed and aggressive, before it splashes away
                through wooden gates, one lock to another
            to feed the entire island.

4.

East India

Once past the food stalls
and balding ticket vendor in his hand-painted kiosk,
you walk a wide lawn to the stone Sun Chariot,
its huge wheels spinning cosmic time
      into human cycles of days and months.

Amid rushing families,
each with a grandmother wrapped in diaphanous silk
and look-alike in-laws replicating the Bollywood pantheon,
      you wander with barefoot girls wearing gold,
their men cocked to tiny pocket phones,

and perhaps attach yourself to a guide
always onward indicating with white kerchief,
   moving children quickly past the softly-chiseled lovers,
who, arched in ritual feast, bangles broken, anklets kicked off,
   bend and join in impossible poses—
love-scratched, joy driven, one into another,
no boundary, no ego
      dissolved into higher consciousness:

Ourselves as we might be, reworked
by master chisels: no shame, no suspicion,
   mesmerized, undressed,
        worthy of the world.

IV.

Facing High Water

Though harsh frost has whitened a hundred grasses,
deep in the courtyard, one grove of green!

Ch'i-chi (864-937)

The Right Time

Seasons have taken their true place in the sun.
Rain is busy gathering shepherds and beekeepers, plowmen
and weavers to boil the coffee and fry the chiliquiles
around the open hearth of human concern.

Something ticks in the limestone,
ripples through the zenith, and explodes
in seeds blowing from the shaman's hand.
In the circular shell of the caracol, in the steady march
of feet going against tyranny,

green light floods the courtyards,
red shadows slant from doorways. Girl soldiers
with ribboned braids, young widows standing before
bayonets and barbed wire—   it is dark
but the sun hasn't set.

Extraordinary actions are required
if sleep is to wake our dreams.

Chiapas, Mexico

Poem from Moon Hill

An odd thing—
to let poems go in the world,
watch sails billow and seeds fall,
see the wheel churn with transparent spray.

Traces of rag and camphor.
Sun lighting the edges of piled bramble.
Tragic mortality—

Words, deeds
fallen in on themselves.
The human massacre upgraded daily,

while angels disguised as children
leap through the tedium, the tall frames
of the adult world.

In from Afar

Crows count out a song in the breeze.
Sky's empty, head whirling—

All those crowds and numbers,
thoughts driven deep on the night train,
random stanzas splattered from pen.

The darkness, the debris—

I didn't go far, didn't hide the heart,
didn't care if my boots sprang a leak, or the stairs
lost their steps before they reached top.

Felt shoulders rub against me.
Saw old friends in new friends
on the world's other side.

What did I find that I wasn't looking for—

That I was too busy reaching and rejecting
to get to the bottom of things?

That among cracked angels
an empty niche returned my name?

That from a house facing the death camp
came a mother's lullaby?

That the girl from My Lai continues to vanish
and reappear in pollen and chaff?

That Buddha, too,

is part of this vanishing world?

That around the temple bell
blue sky rang?

The Cliffs above Poshouinge

Take a rest among old bones
and finger-smoothed shards, galaxy spinning,
grandson whirling swords under hazy snow peaks.

Nothing's under control—

The four directions shifting,
Confucius weeping in a spider's egg
while uprisings proceed, and heads of state,
black and white in their dictating, refuse any argument.

The children huff and puff
up the zigzag trail, want to return home.
Old guys like me crank it into overdrive, follow clouds
over hoodoos, watch sparks jump from the walking stick.

Set the heart right, the old masters
exclaimed. Shift place without moving.
Leave the mind where you started, let feet do the thinking.

Enough to linger in the wild,
favor blowing sand over stale rhetoric.
While grandson tarries over flaked obsidian,
I'll graze on emptiness between yin and yang,
spit out stale air, draw in the new.

Work Song While Gardening

Rake the path, gather bramble,
burn the babble, turn over a stone that gleams
but never reveals its center.

Catch a blossom between the teeth,
amble the weeds, discover a corkscrew seedling
winged and twirling, one that brings you to all fours.

Come down from the top,
dig at the bottom, chew the debris, roll the sun
around with your tongue.

Unwrap the wire from the gate,
undo the cloud, ungun the hip, unbutton the brain,
wander naked without thought of fame.

Hair on the head,
moss after the rain, pull back the leaves
and the ears begin to sing.

Fold the palms, bow to mortality,
take a dust bath in a deserted cave,
begin at the end, follow the wind.

Mountains are moving,
ploughs are rusting, harbors are flooded,
borders do well ground into powder.

Forget the race,
shoulder the wood, carry water,
heat the tea, plunge into fire.

Polish the mirror,
erase the face, quiet the mind
that talks in sleep.

It's Happened

I'm here already,
fumbling along the banister,
trying to catch the phone before the last ring.
        At last I've lost track, no limits exist.
It's pure transcendental folly, which is to say I'm dying
                        to pollinate your eyes.

Thoughts disembodied,
memory on a long walk, work ethic dragged off by its heels.
Like the wind, I've gone nowhere, passed through
mountains, wrapped around the sea,
                        chanced upon the Morning Star.

Did I achieve harmony,
make it into the Forbidden City?
    My axe is stuck in the chopping block
while the sapsucker goes about his non-attainment
        tatting away at the elm.

Surely someday I'll lose my shadow
in the Forest of Wisdom, as age spots fly from my face
and the inner ear wakes me with triplicating secrets.
But I'll never stop following the extra finger
        into the joyous cleavage of the undercover horizon.

Today I'll throw my socks to the wall
        —if they stick, wash them.
Tomorrow, maybe drive into town with the top down,
use my head to shine a little light back into the universe,
stop for a frito pie in the celestial eatery,
        feel the touch of the waitress take my change.

The road home has no name.
It loops through raked alfalfa and broken chapels
where the sun does a kaleidoscope ballet off broken bottles.
At a yard sale, I stop to inspect moonstones
and macramé, pink dial-telephones
       and a rubber mermaid —and find a child
sleeping in the shade of an apricot tree.

The air is still, the world escaping.
Someone's car keys in the dust at my feet
       will probably fit any lock as I turn in sleep.
The day is large, it's the dream that keeps me awake.
It's as if we've all gathered in a room that barely fits,
       and the fun is about to begin.

Time is Short

Let's put down the top,
turn up a rumba, let the rain wet our wings,
neon dissolve into speed, as we move
particularly close in the seat.

Slide your leg over the gears,
lean into the stars and passing semaphores.
At this speed the brakes have no questions.

My chest is full of flames,
how can you stand to wear clothes?
The moon is dancing, the road has generous ears.

I've given up on hats
and seat belts and liberation from meaning.
Tonight the drive is easy.

I know nothing of love.
I've put out the headlights
and taken both hands from the wheel.

Browsing a Bookstore

While browsing a bookstore in an unfamiliar town,
I discovered myself in an anthology of less-familiar poets,
    read a few pages, then flipped to the rear of the book.
There, in 9-point avant-garde, was my biography:

"Cure doctor brought down from the mountains
by the wind. No degrees, plenty of experience.
Recent books include *Walking Stick Repair Made Easy.*"

The bio claimed my poems were "largely metaphysical
in nature, often written in floating gardens,
or in moments of rapture while raking the corral.
With little time to sit down, " it continued
"and hardly able to afford a desk, this is an author
    who often writes standing on his head."

Impressed that the editors included such minor
but important specifics, I read on:
"When not in his jalapeño patch harvesting new poems,
Brandi spends time as a roving insomniac
        seeking the center of incandescence.

"Formerly a part-time restoration specialist at the Center
for Indecisive Romantics, Brandi learned to juggle early on.
He loves women, black bean tortillas, and recording
small details of life with a camera concealed in his sleeve.

"At it since childhood," the bio concluded,
"never clever or contrived, he met most people by accident,
        avoided foghorns, and crashed where he pleased."

Oxford, Mississippi

Two Poems from the Delta

1.

Delta Blues

Robert Johnson to Yosano Akiko:

> *Baby where you stay*
> *last night? You got your hair all tangled*
> *and you ain't talking right.*

Yosano Akiko to Robert Johnson:

> *Please don't ask what remains*
> *of love. Let our poetry endure*
> *as I tidy my hair.*

2.

Unlikely Blues

Bessie Smith to Dylan Thomas:

> *Kiss me honey, it makes my love come down.*
> *Do just what you did last night.*
> *If you want to hear me rave, sweet sweet daddy*
> *Give me what I crave.*

Dylan Thomas to Bessie Smith:

> *Fog has a bone*
> *He'll trumpet into meat,*
> *Let the soil squeal, and the naked egg*
> *Stand straight.*

> *Clarksdale, Mississippi*

Self Portrait in Central Park

This old painter is done with water gazing,
he wants to take off his grass raincoat, put on his neon sneakers,
walk among people, contemplate the white-winged crossbill
on a thin wire of lingerie.

He's had enough of the empty courtyard,
days without visitors, poems welling up from darkness
known only to pine seedlings. It's time for Theda Bara
naked on a tiger skin, a plate of Sicilian anchovies on toast.

Spiritual cultivation, blah—

This old painter has put down his tubes
of Viridian and Loch Ness Grey, the Myth of Freedom
and the Gateless Gate. He'd like to warm himself
on the steps of the Met, view young tattooed legs
uncrossing as they run for the bus.

So many islands to choose from—
He'll shave, polish his belt buckle, become
credibly flashy, and not think twice as he blows out
the lights and leaves the captain's table.

He'll amble under polished granite
and flowering plum, take all the time he needs
for what's going on, and, when good and ready,
return upriver on a raft,

roll out the silk, point his brush
between sudden storms of heightened recollection,
and remember the world as if he'd just been to a movie
and suddenly walked out.

for Creeley

The pleasure of sitting
with friends, rolling reason
into smoke, going far
without going
anywhere.

Dying is not
what I'm afraid of
you once said. *What I fear*
is remaining alone
after those who helped
locate me in life
are gone.

Now the walls
have crowded in, the table
is far away, the chairs
where everyone sat
are back to back.

Someone's sweeping
up the feast. You've gone
and my thinking
follows no end.

30 March 2005

Looking for Water

in memory, Eric Barker

He entered the room
smelling of the sea and wild fennel, asked
if we were ready for a walk —through creation,
blind fathoms, old world heather.

I wasn't sure what he meant
but liked hearing a man talk that way.

In tide-splattered cords and worn canvas shirt
he began to read in a quavering lilt, fingers fluttering
over the page, eyebrows that wouldn't stay put.

He described the work
of the night tide, the hazards of solitude,
a bath in a cold copper stream.

I noticed his pearly veins,
a mole on his chin keeping time to the beat,
a bare toe poking through his sock. Then lost myself
to the charge of alchemy, phosphors dancing
in dark whorls of kelp.

My head rang like a wave-tossed bell
then settled into a quiet wheel of rain, as this troubadour
all throat and eager heart, peppered his poems with stories.
Like the night he stood naked under the Milky Way
listening to surf pound the rocks, after chasing
wild peccaries from his cabbage patch.

I was eighteen, and a gospel ship
was rocking into my harbor with all the revelation

I needed   —that it was okay to come undone,
go adrift, bump against sheer walls,
drop the net into the unseen.

Poetry, a Conspiracy

Rocking and roiling
until the eaves bust from their hinges—

Poetry function of blood and gathering leaves
without delicacy or academy, in the face of cannons and snares
at work too big for Paradise.

Poetry smoking eyelids, full throttle up to bat, line drive
through the headlines, wearing horseshoes and lace,
under veils, in thongs, revealing it all
      on the beach of unilateral conformity.

Poetry gnostic bellboy up on its heels in the clouds
under the lamp, in a motel room drawer
          rearranging chance in the elevator mirror.

Poetry not to please, dangerous poetry
stepping out of the box to see. Walking antenna 24-hour
journey-in-exile, tell it as it is poetry.

Poetry on the plate opening the pores.
Poetry eat what you see. Resistance poetry to get thin with,
third-eye diet deflating the waistline.

Poetry no easy-slide daily writing exercise—
Poetry ditch digging in work flame like nobody's business.
Poetry ants in the pants, secret feel up,
invisible ink, delicious weapon.

Poetry to see where we've been, to take the next step,
to shake a hand, to pull out the rug.
Poetry, to stay alive.

Do Me Love

Do me love
Tear the rose from dawn
Do me long

Do me on the graves
Spread the burning door
Do me upside down

Do the poor rejections in the rain
Do me strong
Do the sunlit nave all night long

Be animal on me, be teeth
Do the old shack along the tracks
Do me free

Sing my burning thing
Make church of legs
Make night thy day

Speak the longing ache
Make noise of swords
Make deep thy please

Do me lunatic in the sun
Keep me love, up til dawn
Hide my lion in the blaze

Do me far, do me wide
Strip thy star, pass the heat
Shade the leaf

Be fear, be love
Touch me with thy need
Be death, be fire

Trouble heaven with thy thirst
Be sleepy at my side
Let me listen, let me find

Do me love
Do thy taste in mine
Be voice, be heatwave

Be candles for the blind
Strew thy ash, break thy wave
Take madness from the mind

Do me love
Do right from wrong
Ask the ankle from the chain

Take me love, ring thy bell
Be tongue that trembles
Clear my breath with your smile

Do me love from light above
Do me out, do me up
Do me wide, do me slim

Do me love
Do me in.

Tuesday, July 7th

More like a day for Bebop
than Mozart, but there they are, side by side
on the turntable, and I play both. Tadd Dameron
backed by an unnamed singer cresting with euphoric aches,
then giddy and giggling, down on her knees
    backsliding in upward cascades.

And Amadeus, spoon by spoon
into the grinder with those Turkish Dances,
maniacal horns, and cultivated cherubs,
goose feather cheeks and slow golden arrows,
then like a money vault upside down, so modernist
                and perfectly angled on the lawn.

But why deconstruct, call out the slant rhyme,
bring in the blank-verse pinch hitters,
    or cloak the obvious in a chintzy veil?

I'll return to the music,
the rock wall waiting to be dressed
in the morning cool, its free-standing shorthand
a maze of broken syllables, and the neighbor's dog,
with its torn pillow and smell of skunk,
nosing out of the milkweed—

More like a day to keep things unexplained,
get out my clippers, prop up the limping honeysuckle,
put the dawn back to sleep, find a mistake,
    and begin with *that*.

3 in the Afternoon

Too stuffy to work—
Bells ringing, ropes dragging, the kids in the cherry tree
are having a better time than me.

Compost needs turning,
stomach's blocked. Bad cheese, political turmoil,
lottery ticket scratched the wrong way.

Time to get out of the loft—
thunder building, melons in labor, corn on clock springs,
earth rotating backwards, tired of human unpredictability.

It's solstice, cat eating a scrub jay, women mopping
the chapel, the virgin on display.

It's wild out here, I'm free
from paper, didn't realize I had so much body hair.
Birds fly backwards, drunk on their own singing.

Why be a poet? I want to leave the clouds, marry the river.
Money is the root of second helpings.
I want pistachio pudding,

a ticket to the town called Duende
where I can eat on a shoestring, discover a little more detail
when the bar girl bends to clean the tables.

How can I go home the same?
I'd rather fulfill tribal tendencies, saddle up my '53 Pontiac,
crash the embargo, order Sanskrit for lunch,
keep to the wrong side of the road.

I've always feared the next to the last verse.
Paperweight snow machine upside down in my brain.
Brigette Bardot leaning on my tailfin.
Edgar Allen Poe asking me to turn my head and cough.

No, I won't return to the loft, nor find myself
in a beige cardigan beginning the day on hazelnut coffee.
The afternoon's too glorious.

A thin, sequined singer belts it out
in the bandstand. Tex with Jean Harlow,
Desmond Tutu, Celia Cruz.

The sun has its arms out.
Who fears t.v. bloodthirst, manufactured enemy?
I'm ashamed of the 21st century,

I thought we could love—
that rapture was in this year, that I could
use the hands from the clock as a ladder,
climb back into the Garden, let beauty happen,

do a little striptease in the face of the barbarians,
complete my dream without their shadow,
flimsy war cry, beanbag face mask,

death watching forever
within them.

When the Hearth Fire Burns Out

I'll die with light
inside my head, like those guys
in the Sierra Maestra,

filled with rhythm
and revolution.

No nurse, please.
Just an overgrown garden,
paths that stray, a little rain for the stones.

What's left of the sky
can break like bread. And roads
unwandered?

Let them fill the glass
as the sea raises a wave, as the soil
begins to sing.

Letter Written in a Late Winter Storm

A day of snow and sharpened pencils,
envelopes filled with confessions. Neon taverns
that once said yes, a woman bending backwards
       under the rum-drunk moon.

Hers and all uncommunicated secrets
breaking from my dream. You, in passing carriages
rushing to the continent's end, I won't forget you.
       I have more questions—

You, in leaking boots, at desks
banging out words into rusty void of petrified ears.
You, my inside-out shadow hailing the galloping Muse
     in her torn sweatpants and loose shirt of sky.
Here you are, on a day of iced eaves
       insisting that my relentless tale weep.

What day of the hour is it,
what year of the week? I see suspicious rings
inside the sun, the past tense of disorder
rolling from mouths of angry men who occupy the airwaves
without meaning or pause, and forget
      that they are prisoners of their own enemy.

So it is I face high water,
pull up my eyeshade, dim the wick of the pen,
walk to the post office, past open-air barbershops
       and coin-operated gargoyles.

I ride nakedly this clearing wind of questions,
     my tailcoat forced to the ground in the snow,
   my suitcase crossing the world on its own.

Notes to the Poems

"Walking with Frank O'Hara and Po Chü-i"

The quotes are from *The Collected Poems of Frank O'Hara*, edited by Donald Allen, and from *The Selected Poems of Po Chü-i*, translated by David Hinton. Frank O'Hara (1926-1966) embraced the anti-literary tradition of the Dadaists and wrote life-collage poems full of humor, irony, and exuberance. Po Chü-i (772-846) was the master of deceptively simple poems. A keen observer of daily life, his work finds source in a relaxed, spontaneous "idleness"—*wu-wei*—selfless action, nothing doing, everything unfolding.

"Has the Old Homeland Changed?"

The title is from a line in "To the Tune: Bodhisattva's Headdress" by Li Ch'ing-chao (1084-1151), poet and calligrapher; perhaps China's first literary feminist. Version by Sam Hamill, *Crossing the Yellow River: 300 Poems from the Chinese*.

"Weminuche Wilderness, Late August"

"old master Ch'ien" refers to T'ao Ch'ien (365-427). His life as recluse poet/farmer was a form of political protest in the face of a ruthless, unworthy ruling class. The quote is from "Early Spring, Thinking of Ancient Farmers," translated by David Hinton, *The Selected Poems of T'ao Ch'ien*.

"A Dance Hall in Baracoa"

Vicente Aleixandre, born 1898, Sevilla; awarded the Nobel Prize for Literature, 1977. The line quoted is from "The Victorious Sun," translated by Lewis Hyde and David Unger in *A Longing for the Light: Selected Poems of Vicente Aleixandre*.

"Traveling Deeper"

Wang Wei (701-761), T'ang Dynasty poet; also a talented musician and a master painter who founded the Southern School of landscape artists. The quote is from "Two Songs of Autumn Longing," translated by Chang Yin-nan and Lewis C. Walmsley in *Poems by Wang Wei*.

"On Visiting a Taoist Recluse"

Kanchendzonga: 8598 meters; third highest peak in the world; guardian deity of Sikkim. Its name means "Five Treasures of the Snows."

"The Right Time"

Chilaquiles: casserole-like dish made from fried tortilla chips baked with green chili and farm cheese.

Caracol: Spanish, "conch shell." The Zapatista rebels in Chiapas, Mexico, refer to each of their five autonomous zones as a Caracol. The Caracol is organised by a junta, a form of local government made up of elected officials from Zapatista communities. A Mayan legend relates how the gods who created the world didn't have time to finish the sky, so four gods stood at the earth's corners to hold the sky in place. One god held watch, blowing a caracol to waken the others if evil fell upon the earth. Later, men and women were taught how to use the caracol to alert others to evil in the world.

"The Cliffs above Poshouinge"

Poshouinge: a Puebloan village that flourished between 1300 and 1600, Rio Chama watershed, northern New Mexico. Only the rubble of the 700 rooms flanking two large ceremonial plazas survive.

Photo "Crowned at Last" by Ira Cohen

John Brandi grew up in Southern California and was introduced to the High Sierras, the Mohave Desert, and the Big Sur by his parents, who encouraged him toward art and writing. After graduating from California State University, Northridge, he worked as a Peace Corps volunteer in Ecuador, traveled the Andean backbone from southern Chile to the Arctic Circle, and lived in Alaska, Mexico, and the Sierra Nevada foothills of California. In 1971, he moved to New Mexico, where he built a cabin in a remote canyon, raised a family, and founded Tooth of Time Press. Since then, he has worked as a poet in the schools, receiving residencies from the state arts councils of Alaska, Arkansas, Montana, Nevada, New Mexico, and New York. Among his honors, Brandi is a recipient of a National Endowment for the Arts Poetry Fellowship and two Witter Bynner Foundation for Poetry teaching awards. He is also an essayist, haiku writer, exhibiting visual artist, and an ardent world traveler. He has served as a guide for U.S. college students studying in Mexico, Bali, and Java and continues to teach and lecture as an itinerant poet in schools, libraries, universities, private foundations, and museums. John lives with his wife, poet and aikido practitioner Renée Gregorio, in El Rito, New Mexico.